Voices From The Past ✳ ✳ ✳ ✳ ✳ ✳ ✳ ✳ ✳ ✳ ✳

REVOLUTIONARY *W*AR

KATHLYN GAY   MARTIN GAY

Twenty-First Century Books

Brookfield, Connecticut

Twenty-First Century Books
A Division of The Millbrook Press, Inc.
2 Old New Milford Road
Brookfield, Connecticut 06804

Library of Congress Cataloging-in-Publication Data
Gay, Kathlyn.
Revolutionary war / Kathlyn Gay and Martin Gay. — 1st ed.
p. cm. — (Voices from the past)
Includes bibliographical references (p.) and index.
1. United States—History—Revolution, 1775–1783—Juvenile literature.
[1. United States—History—Revolution, 1775–1783.] I. Gay, Martin, 1950– .
II. Title. III. Series: Gay, Kathlyn. Voices from the past.
E208.G38 1995   95–13415
973.3—dc20   CIP
                                                               AC

ISBN 0–8050–2844–7

Printed in the United States of America

10 9 8 7 6 5 4 3 2

Map by Vantage Art, Inc.
Cover design by Karen Quigley
Interior design by Kelly Soong

Cover: *Bunker Hill, 17 June 1775* by H. Charles McBarron
Courtesy of National Guard Heritage Series, Dept. of the Army,
National Guard Bureau, Washington, D.C.

Photo credits

p. 8, 9, 17, 45, 49: The Bettmann Archive; p. 11: *Minuteman 1775* by Don Troiani,
photograph courtesy Historical Art Prints, Southbury, Conn.; p. 12: The Granger
Collection, New York; p. 19: Moorland-Spingarn Research Center; p. 24: *Montreal,
25 September 1775* by H. Charles McBarron, courtesy of National Guard Heritage
Series, Dept. of the Army, National Guard Bureau, Washington, D.C.; p. 28, 36, 37
(both), 42: North Wind Picture Archives; p. 41: George Rogers Clark National
Historic Park; p. 53, 56: Anne S. K. Brown Military Collection/Brown University
Library.

Contents

One	A CALL TO ARMS	7
Two	COMPELLING REASONS	15
Three	REBELS WITH A CAUSE	22
Four	ALL THE KING'S MEN	32
Five	WAR ON THE HOME FRONT	40
Six	THE FINAL ACT	48
Source Notes		57
Further Reading		61
Index		63

Acknowledgments

Some of the research for this series depended upon the special efforts of Dean Hamilton, who spent many hours locating primary source materials and other references on America's wars and sorting out appropriate stories among the many personal accounts available. Especially helpful was his work at the archival library of the University of South Florida at Tampa, researching for Spanish-American War and Civil War narratives. For the *World War I* title in this series, Dean also applied his special talents interviewing several of the few remaining veterans of WW I, obtaining their highly personal recollections, which the veterans allowed us to include. Thanks, Dean.

In addition, we would like to thank Lt. Col. (retired) John McGarrahan for locating narratives about personal experiences in the War of 1812, available in the archives at the Lilly Library, Indiana University, Bloomington, Indiana. We also thank Douglas Gay for obtaining narratives on the battle of Tippecanoe at the Tippecanoe County Historical Association in Lafayette, Indiana. Portions of these accounts are included in the *War of 1812* title in this series.

—*Kathlyn Gay and Martin Gay*

QUEBEC

e Superior

St. Lawrence River

▲ Quebec

Ottowa River

Montreal ▲

ME
(part of MA)

Lake
Huron

Lake Michigan

Lake Ontario

Crown Point ▲

Oriskany ▲

● Fort
Niagara

▲ Fort Ticonderoga

NH

Saratoga ▲
Freeman's
Farm ▲

▲ Bennington

Concord
Lexington
Bunker Hill

MA

Lake Erie

● Fort Detroit

NY

Hudson River

CT

RI

● Newport

White Plains

PA

Morristown ●

Germantown ▲
Brandywine ▲

Princeton ▲

▲ ▲ Monmouth
Trenton

▲ Long Island

Incennes

Ohio River

Appalachian Mountains

Baltimore ●

NJ

DE

MD

Proclamation Line of 1763

VA

Petersburg ●

Atlantic Ocean

▲ Yorktown
▲ Great Bridge

Tennessee River

▲ Guilford
Courthouse

NC

Cowpens ▲

▲ Kings Mountain

Moore's Creek Bridge ▲

Camden ▲

Wilmington ●

SC

Chattahoochee River

GA

▲ Charleston

Savannah ▲

FL

Battle

☐ The 13 Colonies

☐ Other British
Territories

300 Miles

300 Kilometers

Date	Battle
April 19, 1775	Lexington & Concord, MA
May 1775	Fort Ticonderoga, NY
May 1775	Crown Point, NY
June 17, 1775	Bunker Hill, MA
Nov. 13, 1775	Montreal, Can.
Dec. 9, 1775	Great Bridge, VA
Dec. 31, 1775	Quebec, Can.
Feb. 27, 1776	Moore's Creek Bridge, VA
Aug. 27, 1776	Long Island, NY
Oct. 28, 1776	White Plains, NY
Dec. 26, 1776	Trenton, NJ
Jan. 3, 1777	Princeton, NJ
Aug. 6, 1777	Oriskany, NY
Aug. 16, 1777	NY, near Bennington, VT
Sept. 11, 1777	Brandywine, PA
Sept. 19, 1777	Freeman's Farm (First), NY
Oct. 4, 1777	Germantown, PA
Oct. 7, 1777	Freeman's Farm (Second), NY
Oct. 17, 1777	Saratoga, NY
June 28, 1778	Monmouth, NJ
Dec. 29, 1778	Savannah, GA
Feb. 25, 1779	Vincennes, IN
May 12, 1780	Charleston, SC
Aug. 16, 1780	Camden, SC
Oct. 7, 1780	Kings Mountain, SC
Jan. 17, 1781	Cowpens, SC
Mar. 15, 1781	Guilford Courthouse, NC
Oct. 6-19, 1781	Yorktown, VA

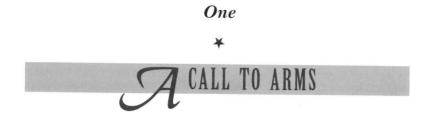

A CALL TO ARMS

In March 1770, Crispus Attucks, a runaway slave who had found a haven in the New England colonies of North America, was part of a taunting crowd brandishing clubs and throwing snowballs at British soldiers. Attucks hit a British officer with a "long cord wood stick . . . either on the soldier's cheek or hat," according to a witness.[1]

When the crowd pressed forward, British soldiers fired, hitting eleven people and killing five, including Attucks, who was later honored as a hero by many colonists. The event, called the Boston Massacre, was often cited as a reason for American colonists to wage war for independence from England.

PROTESTS AGAINST TAXES

As the British added tax after tax to goods shipped to the colonies from British companies, colonists often staged protests and loudly berated British troops sent to protect tax collectors. Because the colonists had no representatives in Parliament, the British national government, to argue their point of view, public protests against unfair taxes continued. In 1773, for example, some colonists known as Patriots or Rebels protested a British tax on tea that was shipped to the

Bostonians objected to unfair taxes and sometimes protested by tarring and feathering a British tax collector.

colonies from the British East India Company. Colonists would not allow the crew to unload their cargo. One night, Patriots disguised as Indians crept aboard the ships and in a few hours threw hundreds of cases of tea into the bay.

This Boston Tea Party, as it became known, led to even greater conflict with England. The British passed harsher laws, banned town meetings, took away the power of local officials, and finally closed Boston Harbor, which prevented goods from going in and out of the city. When people in other colonies heard about the British actions, they sent food and supplies to Boston, signaling their outrage with Britain's heavy-handed authority.

"THE SMELL OF WAR"

For most of his young life, Joseph Martin had heard his family and other American colonists talk about the possibility of

On December 16, 1773, colonists disguised as Indians
raided three British ships anchored in Boston Harbor and
dumped more than 300 chests of tea overboard.

war with Great Britain. Born in 1760, Joseph lived on a farm in the Massachusetts Bay Colony, one of the colonies ruled by the king of England and by Parliament.

Although many of the colonists were from England or were descendants of former British citizens, some resented British rule. Parliament made laws governing much of what went on in the colonies, such as laws that required colonists to pay taxes to England. Since the British had fought many expensive wars to help protect the colonies, the king insisted that colonists pay part of those costs and support a continued military defense.

By 1774, when Joseph Martin turned fourteen, "the smell of war began to be pretty strong," he recalled in a journal. He had no desire to fight and was "determined to have no hand in [a war], happen when it might." As he wrote: "I felt myself to be a real coward. What? Venture my carcass where bullets fly! That will never do for me. Stay at home out of harm's way, thought I, it will be as much to your health and credit to do so."[2]

No doubt Joseph hoped, as many colonists did, that their disputes with England could be settled peacefully. But the British continued to restrict colonists' liberties, and King George III of England ordered more British troops to sail for America to prevent rebellion.

Representatives from each of the colonies met in a Continental Congress in Philadelphia to discuss their problems. Leaders urged each of the colonies to organize a militia, or volunteer army, that would help protect them if a war should break out.

MINUTEMEN AND STATE MILITIA

The British troops that landed in Boston in the spring of 1775 soon learned that colonists had organized volunteers called minutemen, who would respond within minutes if called to defend their property and people. The minutemen had stored weapons in the village of Concord, about 18 miles (29 kilometers) west of Boston.

British soldiers hoped to surprise the minutemen at Concord and capture their weapons. But some colonists who had volunteered to be lookouts knew the soldiers were coming; the lookouts, among them the now famous Paul Revere, raced on horseback to warn the minutemen.

A typical minuteman. Minutemen were a group of volunteers organized to defend the colonists against the British.

In Concord and the nearby town of Lexington, minutemen fought the British in two skirmishes that marked the beginning of the American Revolution. After those battles, urgent calls went out for farmers and townspeople to join their state militias. Joseph Martin recalled, "I was ploughing in the field about half a mile from home, about the twenty-first day of April, when all of a sudden the bells fell to ringing and three guns were repeatedly fired in succession down in the village; . . . I set off to see what the cause of the commotion was."

Joseph found a large group had gathered, most of them men ready to enlist. The enticement was "a dollar deposited upon the drum head [which] was taken up by someone as

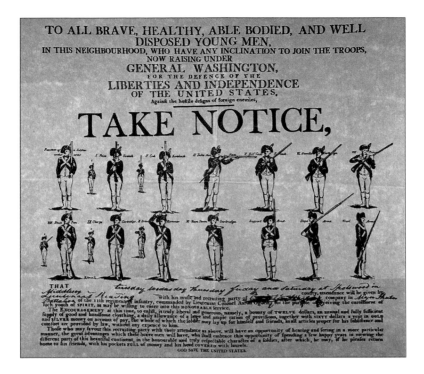

An American Revolutionary War poster calling for volunteers to join General Washington

soon as it was placed there, and the holder's name taken, and he enrolled with orders to equip as soon as possible," Joseph reported. "O, thought I, if I were but old enough to put myself forward, I would be in the possession of one dollar, the dangers of war to the contrary not withstanding."[3]

Eventually, Joseph became part of the military in a brief enlistment, which he called "a priming" before taking on "the whole coat of paint for a soldier."[4] Later he joined as a "regular" and served a six-year tour of duty.

Only a month after Joseph made his first attempt to become part of the militia, leaders of the colonies met in a Second Continental Congress, trying to find a way to make peace with England. At the same time, the Congress knew that the colonies had to be prepared to protect themselves. So they voted to organize a Continental army, with General George Washington in charge.

Even before the American army could take shape, 16,000 militiamen were called to Breed's Hill, mistakenly named Bunker Hill, across the bay from Boston, where they planned to safeguard the city as British soldiers moved in to attack. The militia held the hill for a time but ran out of gunpowder. Although the colonists were defeated in the first major battle of the war, the British suffered great losses. One thousand British soldiers died, more than double the number the militia lost.

BUILDING AN ARMY

Those who battled the British at Bunker Hill and earlier at Concord and Lexington included some free blacks and slaves, who were praised for their heroic efforts. However, many colonists protested the practice of enlisting black soldiers, no matter how brave. White slave owners, including General Washington, feared that blacks who took up arms would revolt, so Washington ordered recruiters not to take blacks into the army. The Continental Congress agreed with the order that all "Negroes be excluded from the new enlistment" and that slaves be "rejected altogether."[5]

The British, though, were eager to recruit blacks and offered freedom to those who would bear arms for the king of England. Members of the Continental Congress worried that large numbers of blacks would be encouraged to fight for the enemy. The Congress also knew the army needed many recruits, so the policy of excluding blacks was reversed. Slaves were promised freedom at the end of their term of service, and free blacks were offered cash to enlist. About 5,000 black soldiers served in segregated units in the Revolutionary War, fighting on land and sea. Many died so the new nation could be independent, but only a few blacks won their freedom after the war was over.

In all, an estimated 290,000 Americans fought in the war for independence, which lasted eight years and extended from the Canadian border in the north to Georgia in the south. Some 4,000 died in the Revolutionary War. These numbers are small compared to those who fought and died in later wars, but the pain and suffering were not minimized. In fact, the Revolution, which was America's first civil war, created deep divisions among colonists and within families. Although American leaders had signed a Declaration of Independence from England, many colonists were uncomfortable with that action and some were resolutely opposed to it.

Two

★

COMPELLING REASONS

*P*art of the Declaration of Independence states that a government derives its "just powers from the consent of the governed," and "whenever any form of government becomes destructive . . . it is the right of the people to alter or abolish it." The declaration underscores some of the reasons why some colonists—among them young people from nine or ten years old to teenagers—marched off to war. They no longer wanted to be ruled by England. Known as Patriots or Rebels, these colonists strongly favored a new form of government and a separate, independent nation.

DIVIDED LOYALTIES

More than half of the colonists, however, wanted no change in the way things were operating. Even though they despised the way England was treating them, the idea of war was even more repulsive.

Some who disliked British rule found that taking sides against Britain was, nevertheless, painful. This was reflected in a letter written by Lydia Post to her husband, Edward, who had gone to fight for the Patriot cause. Lydia tried to explain why her father, a minister who was born in England, was "agitated" about the Rebel actions:

He is attached to the land of his adoption [America], and can sympathize in her distress, but naturally his first, his dearest affections, were given to the land of his birth. Can we censure this? ... Oh no! I honor my father for the sentiment. Do not condemn it, Edward. We love this, our native land.... Her cause seems to us a righteous one. She is over-taxed, oppressed, insulted; my father feels this, he is indignant at it.... [The English] seem ... the foes of our own household to him; brother lifting up sword against brother, in unnatural warfare, which he prays may speedily come to an end![1]

Colonists called Loyalists or Tories favored the British side. Even if they were concerned about injustices, they could see no compelling reason to abandon a monarchy (a government led by a king or a queen) that had existed for hundreds of years. During the Revolutionary War, about 100,000 persons went into exile. Some went to England, others to the Caribbean or to Florida, which was under Spanish rule, while at least half went to Canada.

Tories who stayed in the colonies sometimes were forced to declare whether they were "on the side of the King or for the people [Rebels]," wrote one young Loyalist, Elizabeth Johnston. In her journal, Elizabeth recalled that "if a Tory refused to join the people, he was imprisoned, and tarred and feathered. This was a terrible indignity, the poor creature being stripped naked, tarred all over, and then rolled in feathers."[2]

PROMOTING THE CAUSE

With a relatively small percentage of colonists willing to risk a break with England, the rebellion might have ended quickly. But there were hundreds of colonists who produced speeches, pamphlets, posters, newspaper articles, letters, plays, and songs promoting the Rebel cause. Three men, now well-known historical figures, played a major role in this effort: Samuel Adams, Patrick Henry, and Thomas Paine.

Samuel Adams, a Harvard graduate and a master politician, wrote essays about the natural rights of people. Elected to the Massachusetts legislature, he was tireless in his push for a confrontation with British authority. After the Boston Massacre in 1770, Adams exploited the incident, using it to convince people to side against the British. He helped create broadsides (large posters or banners) that appeared throughout Boston, accusing the British soldiers of atrocities and blaming the problems of the colonies on the king of England.

Adams was one of the organizers of the Sons of Liberty, a group of political activists. Historians believe Adams

Samuel Adams was very active in the push for independence from Britain.

prompted the group to start the Boston Tea Party. Rebels respected him as a leader, but to the king's men he was a dangerous traitor.

Patrick Henry had already been called a traitor when he was a young delegate to the Virginia legislature. He had advocated the repeal of the Stamp Act, one of the British laws that placed a tax on many items colonists used in their daily lives.

A farmer and lawmaker, Henry had a gift for oratory and could transfix an audience. He continually spoke out for Patriot demands, delivering a dramatic speech in 1775 calling for the use of Virginia's militia against England. He did not leave a written record of that now famous speech, but some who heard him wrote down what they recalled. According to one biographer, Henry "commenced somewhat calmly," but soon "his voice rose . . . until the walls of the building . . . seemed to shake and rock."[3]

Over and over, Henry likened the British rule to slavery for colonists. "Is life so dear or peace so sweet as to be purchased at the price of chains?" he asked his audience. As Henry neared the end of his speech, he extended both his arms aloft, "his voice swelled to its boldest note of exclamation," and he cried, "Give me liberty, or give me death!"[4]

Parts of Henry's speech were repeated throughout the colonies, which did much to arouse the people. Even if colonists did not hear Henry's words, they were likely to soon read pamphlets written by a new immigrant from England, Thomas Paine.

Paine did with his pen what Patrick Henry did with his oratory. After arriving in the American colonies in late 1774, Paine embraced the new ideas of Adams and Henry. He wrote like a man possessed. In 1776, Paine anonymously published a pamphlet titled *Common Sense*, pointing out that it was a matter of common sense for colonists to separate themselves from a repressive government. At least 500,000 colonists eventually purchased the pamphlet, and by all accounts Paine's words changed almost all who read them. Even years later, near the end of the war, a Rebel soldier noted that he and others toasted "the Congress of the year 1776 & common Sence."[5] Many believe that the inspired writings of Thomas Paine encouraged the Rebels to remain loyal to the revolution.

CONTINUING THE PROPAGANDA CAMPAIGN

Others not so well known also played important roles in the campaign for freedom. Some colonists wrote plays and political satires against England. Others published poetry advocating freedom. Among the poets was Phillis Wheatley, a young girl brought as a slave from Africa when she was only eight years old. Some of her poems pointed out her love of freedom and compared slavery to the condition of colonists under British rule.

Phillis Wheatley was a black slave who wrote poetry mainly during the time of the Revolutionary War. She was the first to use the name Columbia, *in honor of Christopher Columbus, to describe the new nation that was to become the United States.*

People also held meetings and listened to speakers from the immediate area. Every region seemed to have its own champion of liberty. Although pamphlets were widely distributed among the colonies, local newspapers played a prominent role in spreading news about the war and persuading people to support the Rebels.

Paper shortages were a major difficulty, however. After the start of the war, Britain stopped the export of paper stock for newspaper printing. But that did not deter Mary Goddard, a publisher of several papers and a staunch advocate of the Patriot cause. She built a paper mill to guarantee her own source of newsprint. Her newspaper, which was the first to print the text of the Declaration of Independence with all the signers' names, could usually be published even when others could not.

Yet Goddard encountered obstacles. As she noted in one issue, "The stoppage of the PAPER-MILL, near this Town, for the want of a Supply of Rags, and the enormous prices demanded at the Stores here for Paper, constrains us to print the MARYLAND JOURNAL on this dark and poor sort."[6]

This resourceful woman knew the importance of the printed word. If the presses stopped, persuasive messages might not reach the people, and colonists might lose their will to fight for the cause.

A FAVORITE SONG

While many colonists were inspired by the newspaper articles, pamphlets, broadsides, and speeches, they also were bolstered by patriotic songs. Dozens of war songs were written and sung, providing an emotional boost for the soldiers in the fields and the sailors on ships as well as their loved ones at home.

The favorite American song by far was "Yankee

Doodle." Fifers played the tune, and soldiers and citizens sang it, often changing the verses. The song was so pervasive that British soldiers, known as redcoats, tried to mock the Americans by playing it at Lexington and Concord when they marched there.

But Americans gloried in "Yankee Doodle." It became the battle cry for the Patriots.

Three

★

REBELS WITH A CAUSE

John Greenwood probably played "Yankee Doodle" hundreds of times. From early childhood, he had loved the fifers and drummers marching with military units around his Boston home. He learned to play the fife and was an able performer by age ten, the year he joined a Massachusetts militia company under Captain Martin Gay. By the time hostilities began, John was a five-year veteran—at fifteen years of age.

Events had moved very quickly after the battles at Concord and Lexington. The British occupied Boston, one of the most important colonial cities. General Washington, who took charge of the American forces on July 3, 1775, ordered a siege of Boston soon afterward.

John took his place with the other Rebels. Their mission was to keep supplies from the occupying British troops. As John recalled an incident at Bunker Hill:

> The English were so penned up in Boston that they could get no fresh provisions except what they stole from the poor unprotected inhabitants near the seashore. . . . On one occasion they came over to steal some cows . . . but were immediately perceived by our people, who quickly marched down toward them. . . . Just as we had crossed the bridge our men were exposed to the fire from the British fort at

Bunker Hill. . . .As eight or ten of us were in a huddle running up the hill, a [cannon] ball . . . struck about three feet from me, driving the dirt smack in our faces. . . . [The British] did not take anything with them, however, and only stabbed two or three cows with their bayonets.

AN ATTACK ON CANADA

Although the British paid dearly for their gains at Bunker Hill, they held Boston and controlled the seas, landing thousands of troops to put down the rebellion. The Americans had to act swiftly.

Soon after Bunker Hill, the Continental Congress authorized an attack on Canada. Washington directed his troops to Quebec to capture and control the province so that no British or Tory offensive would come from that direction. He also feared that Native Americans would attack. Although some Native Americans fought for or assisted the Rebels, many northern Indian tribes became British allies because of their anger against colonists who had taken their land.

The Continental army marched through the northeastern wilderness, which was rugged, wooded terrain with rivers and lakes to cross. Cold weather and scarce food supplies added to the difficulties. One of the soldiers, John Joseph Henry, noted that they "took up the line of march through a flat and boggy ground" and later "arrived by a narrow neck of land at a marsh which was appalling. It was three-fourths of a mile over, and covered by a coat of ice, half an inch thick."[2]

John Joseph's company included two women—wives of soldiers who, like numerous others during the war, accompanied their husbands to the camps and sometimes to the battlefield. One of the women turned back to search for her husband, who had fallen behind and later died. The other

Americans fought the British in Canada but never captured Quebec. Northern Indians sided with the British because they thought Americans were taking their land.

woman went on through the marsh as the soldiers broke "the ice here and there with the butts of [their] guns and feet," the company tramping "waist deep in the mud and water."[3]

In spite of tremendous grit and heroism, the Patriots never captured Quebec. Colonel Benedict Arnold, who later became a turncoat and sided with England, led the attack on the city. He was forced to retreat in early 1776. After that, the next major thrust of the war was near Boston, which the

British evacuated, and in the area to the south around New York and New Jersey.

DEFEAT AT LONG ISLAND

General Washington decided that the British army's most likely point of attack would be New York, so he ordered troops to fortify the city and the surrounding islands. Patriots came from New England, the West, and Canada to aid in the defense. Young Lieutenant Benjamin Tallmadge of Connecticut was among the 10,000 men who crossed the East River at Brooklyn. He reported that "on the 27th of August, the whole British army . . . to the number of 25,000 men, with the most formidable train of field artillery, landed near Flatbush . . . and moved toward Jamaica and Brooklyn."[4]

A ferocious battle followed, which Captain Enoch Anderson described:

> The British pressed hard upon us with far superior numbers. . . . I was wounded,—a bullet struck me on the chin and run down into my neck. Many fell. . . . Some men were lost. . . . A hard day this, for us poor Yankees! Superior discipline and numbers had overcome us. A gloomy time it was, but we solaced ourselves that at another time we should do better.[5]

But that time would not come at Long Island. The British had surrounded the American forces and they were closing in; Washington had to retreat.

A LUCKY FOG

Benjamin Tallmadge described the great risk that Washington undertook to get out of the redcoats' noose:

To move so large a body of troops ... across a river a full mile wide, with rapid current, in the face of a victorious, well disciplined army nearly three times as numerous as his own ... seemed to present the most formidable of obstacles. But in the face of these difficulties, the Commander-in-Chief so arranged his business that ... troops began to retire from the lines in such a manner that ... as one regiment left their station on guard, the remaining troops moved to the right and left and filled up the vacancies. ...

As the dawn of the next day approached ... a very dense fog began to rise, and it seemed to settle in a peculiar manner over both encampments.[6]

That lucky fog was the finishing touch on a bold and clever plan. Washington ordered the retreat as the only way to save his army from certain capture or destruction. In fact, the war might have ended at Long Island but for what a citizen at home, Lydia Post, felt was divine intervention. With obvious excitement, she wrote to her husband about the events that saved the army:

Today received intelligence of the unfortunate affair of Brooklyn. What a skillful movement was that of General Washington—a wonderful retreat!—the enemy so near that the sound of their pickaxes and shovels could be heard! It is a new proof of his cool forethought and judgment. The heavy fog seemed to fall providentially. May we not accept it as an omen that our leader is the favored of heaven?[7]

THE RETREAT THROUGH NEW JERSEY

Favored or not, Washington and his officers needed a plan to prevent a total loss. Fortunately, the British forces did not press their advantage, and the Continentals gained some breathing room. They also were able to move steadily north, but again they experienced defeat—at places named Harlem Heights, White Plains, and Fort Washington. Eventually, the main body of Washington's men made it to a crossing of the Delaware River at Trenton, New Jersey, which Captain Anderson recounted:

> It was dusk before we got to Trenton. Here we stayed all night. In the afternoon of the next day, we crossed the Delaware into Pennsylvania, and in two hours afterwards the British appeared on the opposite bank and cannonaded us; but we were in the woods and bushes and none were wounded that I heard of.
>
> The night we lay amongst leaves without tents or blankets, laying down with our feet to the fire. It was very cold. We had meat, but no bread. We had nothing to cook with, but our ramrods, which we run through a piece of meat and roasted it over the fire, and to hungry soldiers it tasted sweet.[8]

The redcoats and the Hessian soldiers that they hired to fight for them were content to stay the winter on the New Jersey side. Along with the cold weather and lack of supplies, there were reasons enough for Washington to rest his men in the wilds of Pennsylvania. The situation was grim, and on December 17, the commander in chief was nearly without hope.

TURNING THE TABLES

Desperate for a victory to turn the tide of the war, Washington planned a sneak attack on the Hessian garrison. On Christmas night, he crossed the ice-choked Delaware River in a driving sleet- and snowstorm. His attack came as a total

*Hessian soldiers could be easily identified by the
tall hats that were part of their uniforms.*

surprise to the Hessian commander, Colonel Johann Rall,
who thought that the Rebels were "almost naked, dying of
cold, without blankets, and very ill supplied with provisions."[9]

Rall's assessment was correct, but he failed to take into
account the spirit of soldiers like John Greenwood, who had
just arrived from the Canadian campaign. John's account of
the fighting of December 26, 1776, showed his courage:

> None but the first officers knew where we were going or
> what we were going about, for it was a secret expedition. . . .

As we advanced, it being dark and stormy so that we could not see very far ahead, we got within 200 yards of about . . . 400 Hessians who were paraded, two deep, in a straight line with Colonel Rall, their commander, on horseback. . . . They made a full fire on us, but I did not see that they killed any one. . . .

As we had been in the storm all night we were wet through and through ourselves . . . our guns and powder were wet also, so that I do not believe one would go off . . . and, although there was not more than one bayonet to five men, orders were given to "Charge bayonets and rush on!" and rush on we did. Within pistol-shot they again fired point blank at us; we dodged and they did not hit a man . . . they broke in an instant and ran like so many frightened devils into the town. . . . General Washington, on horseback and alone, came up to our major and said, "March on, my brave fellows, after me!" and rode off.[10]

The next day, John's enlistment was up and he started back to Boston. His comrades, who were left to carry on, took stock of their great victory: Rall had been killed in the attack, and the Hessians quickly surrendered. The battle, which lasted less than an hour, accounted for about a thousand prisoners and just five American casualties. Two of the American soldiers had frozen to death.

Victory included the capture of much needed supplies to reoutfit the weary Continental troops. Throughout the army and the colonies, spirits were at an all-time high. But conditions were still pitiful, and men who had completed their enlistments wanted to return home.

General Washington pleaded with his troops to stay on and solidify the gains they had made by taking Trenton. But no one stepped forward to volunteer. A sergeant who was there recounted how General Washington urged his men to carry on:

The General wheeled his horse about, rode in front of the regiment and addressing us again said, "My brave fellows, you have done all I asked you to do, and more than could be reasonably expected; but your country is at stake, your wives, your houses and all that you hold dear. . . . If you will consent to stay one month longer, you will render that service to the cause of liberty and to your country which you probably never can do under any other circumstances."

A few stepped forth, and their example was immediately followed by nearly all who were fit for duty in the regiment.[11]

With those men, Washington directed a march toward Princeton, where the sergeant noted that "the ground was literally marked with the blood of the soldiers' feet" as the men "were without shoes and other comfortable clothing."[12] The battle took place on January 3, 1777, before the surprised British could reinforce the city.

Washington and his troops placed the city and most of New Jersey firmly under control of the Continental army. The general then took his tired forces to an encampment at Morristown, where he planned to spend the winter waiting for new recruits to come.

REINFORCEMENTS

In the spring, fresh troops arrived regularly at the camp near Morristown. Among them was Jeremiah Greenman, who had served in Canada after his enlistment at the age of eighteen. Now an experienced soldier, he came with many others to reinforce the main army. He observed in his diary that it was a "very unwholesum time . . . very sickly. the men comes into town from head quarters . . . very plenty smallpox."[13]

Soldiers in other battles suffered similar hardships, and

many never survived the diseases and near starvation, not to mention the musket and cannon fire. Sixteen-year-old Ebenezer Fletcher was one who nearly made the ultimate sacrifice. Right after he enlisted, his regiment, under the command of Colonel Nathan Hale at Fort Ticonderoga in New York, was forced to march because the British were ready to attack. Ebenezer was in poor shape, however. As he explained:

> Having just recovered from the measles, and not being able to march with the main body, I fell in the rear.... Just as the sun rose, there was a cry, "the enemy are upon us." . . . Orders came to lay down our packs and be ready for action. The fire instantly began.... Every man was trying to secure himself behind girdled trees.... I made shelter for myself and discharged my piece. Having loaded again and taken aim, my piece missed fire. I brought the same a second time to my face; but before I had time to discharge it, I received a musket ball in the small of my back, and fell with my gun cocked....
>
> I . . . crawled about two rods [33 feet] among some small brush, and got under a log.... I was not discovered by the enemy till the battle was over.... I heard one of them say, "Here is one of the rebels." I lay flat on my face across my hands, rolled in my blood.... They soon came to me, and pulled off my shoes, supposing me to be dead. I looked up and spoke, telling them I was their prisoner, and begged to be used well.

Ebenezer's life was spared and, as he stated, "I was treated as well as I could expect."[14] Eventually, he recovered from his wounds and managed to escape from the British, rejoining his company to fight another day.

Four

ALL THE KING'S MEN

The British were not eager to fight this war against an "enemy" that spoke the same language and came from the same traditions. In addition, a war would ruin a profitable overseas trade that had been benefiting British merchants for a hundred years. In the view of many, America was a far-off place better left alone.

Because so few Britains wanted to risk their lives across the ocean, the government had to take drastic action, offering good pay and other benefits to those who would join His Majesty's troops. Such rewards may have tempted fifteen-year-old John Shaw, who suffered from hard times and a difficult family life. He left his home near Yorkshire and went to Cloverly, where the Royal Army was stationed. He kept a journal of his experiences, writing:

> No sooner had I entered the town than, to my great joy, I met one of the 33rd regiment's recruits, who, when I told him my business, gladly gave me his hand and said, "Come, my fine lad, the king wants soldiers; come on, my fine boy, I'll shew you the place where the streets are paved with pancakes; and where the hogs are going through the streets carrying knives and forks on their backs, and crying *who will come and eat?*" [1]

John went with a sergeant to see a superior officer, one Captain Carr, who continued the interview:

> "Well, my lad," says the captain, "how old are you?" Fifteen or sixteen. "Well, sergeant, bring the standard;" which being brought I measured five feet and one inch high, without my shoes. "Well, my lad," says the captain, "you are too low and under size, and I cannot take you; but here is a shilling and I'll give you a new hat ... and a new suit of clothes, and go home and be a good boy, and go to school, and come to me two or three years hence, and I will enlist you." ... "No," said I, "if you will not take me, I will go and enlist [as] a drummer." ... "Well then," said the captain, "since the lad is determined to be a soldier, and appears to be a promising youth, I will take him, and here are three guineas, and a crown to drink his majesty's health; now, my fine lad, be a good boy, and I will take you to be my waiter." [2]

As a young recruit, John crossed the ocean with thousands of other redcoats to fight in the war. But not all the soldiers were from England. The Royal Army was so desperate for fighting men that the king sought help from German royalty. Several German princes agreed, for a fee, to send some of their troops to fight the war in place of British subjects. Thirty thousand of these Hessian mercenaries—hired soldiers—went to America.

A MERCENARY FORCE

One of the Hessians was Valentin Asteroth, an eighteen-year-old chaplain's assistant who kept a diary of his experiences, beginning with the long voyage to America. Valentin left England in early June of 1776, but he did not arrive in New York until late October:

There for the first time in 22 weeks I touched land again. In that region all the people had fled. The houses stood empty. We satisfied our hunger with apples and then entered a small house. There we found three Negroes. They were reserved. We obtained wholesome potatoes from them, but they could not understand us, nor we them.[3]

While Washington's troops wintered in Morristown, Valentin's division was sent by ship to Rhode Island harbor, where the Rebels

had taken the precaution of fortifying the city and the harbor with three forts.... It seemed impossible for us to capture the city. However, our admiral . . . took us into an impassable harbor which the rebels thought could not be entered. When they saw us and saw our fleet enter, there was a great outcry and they fled to Providence with bag and baggage ... they had heard such tales about us, that we were not human, we plundered everyone, and burned and killed everything and everyone in our path. Therefore, these rebels were happy to run from us even in their great fear.[4]

THE CANADIAN PLAN

In early 1777, the British decided on a new attack plan hatched by a general known as "Gentleman Johnny" Burgoyne. The plan called for the isolation of New England from the rest of the colonies. Over several months, Burgoyne brought together a large contingent of troops. They included British and Hessian infantry and artillery, 400 Indians, and some Tory and Canadian fighters. Burgoyne led the troops south through the wilderness of New York. He intended to meet with two other armies, an action that, he was certain, would effectively divide the rebels and end the fighting. But the plan was easier to complete on paper than in real life.

The massive British force of over 7,000 men with 138 large guns sailed south on Lake Champlain, eventually surprising the Americans at New York's Fort Ticonderoga in July. The Rebel troops were forced to retreat, setting fires to cover their flight. But the British forces pursued, through forests, across lakes and rivers, and over mountains. They built roads and bridges as they traveled, and carried most of their supplies on their backs because they had few horses and carts. One Hessian officer wrote a letter home describing the "d——d hard task" of advancing: "It was August, in the hottest part of the year, and one could hardly breathe when sitting still in the tents; dysentery raged among us, but we had to work to maintain life."[5]

Great battles took place at Bennington, Vermont, and Brandywine, Pennsylvania, as summer turned to autumn, and a critical confrontation at Saratoga, New York, was on the horizon. Burgoyne camped near Saratoga to await the arrival of another British army under Sir Henry Clinton. But Clinton's army did not arrive from the southwest as expected, and Burgoyne was surrounded.

BURGOYNE'S DEFEAT AT SARATOGA

In the fall of 1777, a massive force of Americans under General Horatio Gates pounded Burgoyne's camp with heavy fire, and the British troops suffered greatly. So did the family of Baroness von Riedesel, who was traveling with her husband, a Hessian commander under Burgoyne, and their three small daughters. The baroness wrote in her journal on October 9, 1777:

> I was wet through and through by the frequent rains, and
> was obliged to remain in this condition the entire night, as I
> had no place whatever where I could change my linen. I
> therefore, seated myself before a good fire, and undressed

my children; after which, we laid down together upon some straw. . . . I asked [an officer] . . . why we did not continue our retreat while there was yet time, as my husband had pledged to cover it and bring the army through.

"Poor woman," answered he, . . . "have you still the courage to wish to go further in this weather? Would that you were only our commanding general! He halts because he is tired, and intends to spend the night here and give us a supper."[6]

Within a week, conditions became so intolerable for Burgoyne that he was forced to surrender. The defeat at Saratoga was a tremendous blow. In all, an estimated 5,000 to 6,000 men surrendered. More important, the French, who had been watching this civil war with growing interest, decided in February 1778 to sign an agreement officially supporting the colonies in their attempt to overthrow the king's rule.

General Burgoyne, commander of a British force from Canada, surrendered to General Gates at Saratoga on October 17, 1777.

General Washington welcomed the news of the French alliance. The British had occupied Philadelphia, and Washington had led his troops to Valley Forge, Pennsylvania, where they had set up camp in severe winter weather. There was little food or clothing and poor shelter—only log huts. Thousands were without blankets and shoes. Frostbite, starvation, and smallpox killed hundreds of soldiers. Yet under these intolerable conditions, Washington kept his army together, and with the help of several generals from Europe, he was able to train and drill his troops into a better fighting force.

General Washington's soldiers were poorly equipped to withstand the harsh winter at Valley Forge.

This is the interior of a reconstructed army hut that provided some shelter for the troops at Valley Forge.

With the French aiding the Rebel cause, the British were not sure how they were going to maintain a fight against the colonists on the ground and the French on the high seas. England suggested many compromises to end the war. But the colonists wanted only independence, which the British refused. Stubbornly, the British turned their attention to the southern colonies, where they had support from many Tory volunteer militias. They made gains, taking Georgia, then, less than a year later, handing the Americans their harshest defeat at Charleston, South Carolina.

The British forces did not advance easily, however. Like the Rebels, they were in constant need of supplies. They had to be resourceful to find food among the residents of the land they tried to capture. John Shaw, who fought with the British in the southern campaign, told how he was "impelled by hunger" and with another soldier went in search of food one day:

> I proceeded forward about three or four miles, until we came to a fine open plantation, and an elegant framed house belonging to a major Bell of the American army. So we entered the house, where we found, an old lady and her two daughters—we saluted them with as much politeness as our awkward manners would admit of; and the old lady very civilly asked us to sit down.—We soon told her ... that we wanted some flour; upon which she immediately filled our knapsacks, and invited us to stay 'till something could be made ready, which invitation we readily accepted; and I very well remember that I got some of the best Johnny-cake [flat corn bread] I ever ate in my life.[7]

While the soldiers ate, the woman of the house tried to convince the two redcoats to defect for the Rebel cause. She even offered her "two daughters, and a complete suit of clothes a piece" if they would join up. But the British soldiers feared "the bad consequences of desertion, that it was death by the laws of war . . . a thing not much desired." However, Shaw admitted, "If I could have entertained the smallest hopes of succeeding in gaining the affections of either of the young ladies, so lovely were they in my eyes, that I would cheerfully have hazarded my life and taken the old lady at her word."[8]

The two redcoats left the plantation as soon as they had finished eating, but they had hardly "gone half way up the lane" when they saw seven Continental army officers on horseback advancing toward them. Shaw recounted that he and his buddy "concluded to go and meet them . . . and falling to our knees begged for quarter; which they granted us and said, 'come on, we will give you good quarters;' and so we went past the house that had betrayed us—it was fine fun for the old lady to see how handsomely she had tricked us."[9]

Five

★

WAR ON THE HOME FRONT

The woman who helped Rebel soldiers capture the two redcoats was just one of many citizens left at home to tend to the businesses, farms, and families. Whether they were Patriot or Tory, they faced daily challenges. Supplies were low, and prices of almost all goods were inflated beyond the reach of the average person. And there was always the risk that the enemy would take whatever was wanted from the defenseless.

That risk was especially great on the western front, in the Northwest Territory that included what is now Kentucky, Indiana, Illinois, and Michigan. Numerous stories—some exaggerated, others based on fact—described how settlers were violently attacked by the Iroquois, who were encouraged and paid by the British to raid frontier settlements. George Rogers Clark, a young woodsman, gained fame for the expeditions that he led to fight the British and their Indian allies in the West. However, Clark was able to persuade some Indian tribes to support his cause, and others joined the French who aided the colonists.

Colonists in the East seldom knew about the action on the frontier, because news traveled slowly. Moreover, most of the Revolutionary War was fought in New England and along the Atlantic Coast, where people like Lydia Post, at home

In the summer of 1778, George Rogers Clark offered Indian tribes north of the Ohio River a choice of two belts— red for war against the Americans or white for neutrality and peace.

with her father and children, were more concerned about protecting themselves and their property. Lydia told how mercenaries with the British forces took supplies from the Posts' neighbors:

> The Hessians have been ordered to cut down all the saplings they can find. They pile them along the road about twelve feet high, then by pressing teams and wagons, they cart it away to forts and barracks at a distance. It is a serious loss; in a few years our farms will be without wood for use. They (the Hessians) burn an immense quantity;—even the rail fences, unless we take care to cut and cart wood for

*British and Hessian soldiers frequently took supplies
and other property from colonists' homes.*

their constant use. Keeping the fire a-going all night, many a
poor farmer rises in the morning to find his cattle strayed
miles away, or his grain trampled down and ruined![1]

OCCUPATION BY CONTINENTAL SOLDIERS

Continental forces also demanded much from citizens, but
most colonists cooperated with Patriot soldiers who needed
food and lodging. Sarah (Sally) Wister, a sixteen-year-old
Quaker girl from Pennsylvania, could not hide her excitement when her aunt's home was occupied by friendly
American troops. In her journal, which began in 1777, she
wrote:

> Cousin Prissa and myself were sitting at thee door I in a green skirt dark short gown, and two genteel men of the military order rode up to the door ... and asked if they could have quarters for General Smallwood. Aunt Foulke thought she could accommodate them.... One of the officers dismounted and wrote Smallwoods quarters over the door which secured us from straggling soldiers, after this he mounted his steed and rode away. When we were alone [our] dress and lips were put in order for conquest.[2]

Although Sally and her cousin primped and prepared to flirt with the soldiers, the excitement of being in the middle of the action could quickly turn to fear and uncertainty once the battle began to rage.

Margaret Morris also kept a journal of the times when her town was occupied by the defending American army. Her home was not used as a barracks, but she often provided food and medical treatment for the men housed among her neighbors. These actions put her and all of the civilians at risk. Margaret described one incident in which a young girl stepped into her home, and a musket "ball met her ... took the comb out of her hair, and gently grazed the skin of her head without doing her any further injury."[3]

TORY EXPERIENCES

In Georgia, where the loyal Tories were more numerous, the Rebels often occupied homes and took over property for the cause. When Elizabeth Johnston was twelve years old, her father and the family farm were nearly seized by American troops. With the help of a slave, her father escaped, dashing out a garden door and hiding in some tall grass. Later Elizabeth's father made it out of the country and into Nova Scotia, Canada, where he joined other Loyalists who had fled persecution by the Patriots.

Although many Loyalists lost their land, Elizabeth helped save her family's property. As she recalled in her journal:

> Commissioners were appointed to [take] the Loyalists' property and dispose of it ... because of their not joining the rebels. ... My grandfather had a petition drawn up which he made me take ... to the Board of Commissioners, which set forth the orphan condition I was left in, and petitioned that my father's property might be given to me. This request I have every reason to think was [granted], as our property was not sold as was that of many other Loyalists.[4]

Grace Galloway's home in Philadelphia was one of those lost. Her husband, Joseph Galloway, was a powerful politician in Pennsylvania in the years leading up to the war. Since Galloway sided with Britain, his life and liberty were endangered. He, too, was forced to flee, while his wife, like many other Loyalist women, stayed to seek help from lawyers, friends, and government officials. But nothing worked for Grace Galloway, and she was ordered to leave her home. According to her diary, one official, a Mr. Peel,

> went Upstairs & brought down My Work bag & 2 bonnets & put them on the side table. ... we went in the entry to sit. ... after we had been in ye Entry some time ... Peel said ye Chariot was ready but he would not hasten me I told him I was at home & in My own House & nothing but force shou'd drive me out of it he said it was not ye first time he had taken a Lady by the Hand ... & as the Chariot drew up Peel fetched My Bonnets & gave one to me ... then with greates[t] air said come ... give me your hand I answer'd indeed I will not nor will I go out of my house but by force. he then took hold of my arm & I rose & he took me to the

door I then Took hold on on[e] side & look[ed] round & said pray take Notice I do not leave my house of My own accord.... Peel said with a sneer very well Madam & when he led me down ye step I said now Mr. Peel let go My Arm I want not your Assistance.... you Mr. Peel are the last Man on earth I wou'd wish to be Obliged to.[5]

A colonist who sided with Britain was called a Loyalist or Tory. Here, a Tory is "drummed out" of his village.

THE ULTIMATE SACRIFICE

While some women fought to maintain their homes or joined troops in the Revolution, sometimes dying beside them, others provided care and humane treatment for wounded and dying soldiers. Many women lost their husbands, sons, fathers, uncles, and other relatives. In a letter to her husband fighting with the Continental army, Lydia Post described some of the horrors that a friend, General Nathaniel Woodhull, had to endure. General Woodhull was stationed at Jamaica on Long Island, where he tried to protect families of American soldiers fighting the advances of the British. Because General Woodhull had only a few men with him, he was overtaken. According to Lydia's lengthy letter, a

> cowardly assassin brutally assaulted the defenseless General with a broad-sword. He would have killed him, but his hand was [stopped] by an officer of more ... honour.
>
> One arm was horribly mangled, from shoulder to hand. In this situation he was dragged from place to place: at length he was ... removed, mangled, bleeding, and parched with fever-heat, to an inn at Jamaica.[6]

While at the inn, the general was cared for by the owner, a Mrs. Hinchman. She not only bandaged Woodhull's wounds but also provided the "best room and bed for the poor wounded General's use." But the next day, the British marched on, taking the general with them. They stopped at a halfway house (a tavern or inn), Lydia reported, and while the soldiers drank and "regaled," they left the general

> with a guard, under the horse-shed! ...The landlady, went out to minister to the weak and fainting patriot ... and invited him with tender pity and solicitude, to partake of some refreshment. The guard impudently asked, "If she had nothing for them?" "I *give* to prisoners, you can *buy*," the kind woman replied.[7]

The journey continued to another town, where the general was taken to a hospital. A surgeon amputated the general's mangled arm, but infection had spread and Woodhull was near death. He asked for his wife, Ruth, and as Lydia put it: "Strange to say, the request was granted." Ruth packed a wagon full of food and other supplies and traveled more than 70 miles (113 kilometers) to the hospital to be with her husband. But she "arrived only in time to receive his dying breath." Ruth then placed her "husband's body in the wagon, and went on her lonely way home." In Lydia's view, Ruth must have found "some comfort in the thought that the precious remains of her gallant husband were not left with the enemy" and that he was buried in "honourable pride, that for his country he had laid down his life."[8]

Six

★

THE FINAL ACT

The winter of 1781 found Washington and his weary army again at Morristown. This time they had less provisions than they had had at Valley Forge. Men were hungry, tired, frostbitten, and unpaid. Some had been forced to stay beyond their agreed time of enlistment. Nathanael Greene, who commanded the troops in the South, sought help from two different colonial legislatures. As Greene explained in a letter to a friend, "The wants of this army are so numerous and various that the shortest way of telling you is to inform you that we have nothing."[1] But Greene's requests were to no avail. The money was not there.

Some soldiers felt mutiny was the only recourse. More than 1,000 troops along with officers from various regiments stationed in Morristown were so disgruntled that they rioted and began a march to the Continental army headquarters near West Point on the Hudson River to lodge their complaints. Some Continental commanders believed the men planned to defect to the British, but that was not their intent; instead they wanted their pay, food, clothing—what was due them. The revolt was eventually put down, and leaders of the mutiny were sentenced to death, but many colonists at the time thought the troops were "only doing themselves justice," according to one account.[2]

No matter what the misery and discontent, Washington had to keep the war effort going. He knew the only way to win now was through naval superiority: something that had not been possible before the French decided to aid the colonists.

PRIVATEERS

At the start of the war, England was the mightiest country in the world because it had the most powerful navy. In contrast, the Second Continental Congress in 1775 had commissioned a navy "with only two armed merchant ships, two armed brigantines and one armed sloop [which] had no precedent in history to make war against such a power as Britain," according to the hero of American naval history John Paul Jones.[3]

This famous painting shows the Bonhomme Richard, *commanded by John Paul Jones, in a battle with the British warship* Serapis *on September 23, 1779. Jones captured the* Serapis, *but his own ship was badly damaged and later sank.*

Though the Continental navy did have some small successes, the real might of the Patriots' power at sea was in the private ships that sailed under commission of the states or the Congress. These privateers were outfitted with guns and men to harass the British and to lend aid to the soldiers on the land. Any prizes captured became the property of the shipowners.

John Greenwood, who had completed his army enlistment, signed up for a tour on one of these vessels, with a crew of 150 operating out of Boston:

> We had orders to cruise off New York, but unfortunately we were blown by a gale of wind into the Gulf Stream....It continued to blow six days and nights and the pumps were kept constantly at work, for with four feet of water in the hold and the ship so old and crazy, we expected to go to the bottom every moment.[4]

Indeed, John was knocked into the dark and stormy sea on the last night of the storm. He was holding on to a gangway rail that gave way. "It was at night, dark as pitch, and they cried out that I was overboard, but I told them I was safe." And once John was back on ship, with the gale subsiding, the captain made a decision to sail for the quieter waters of the West Indies, where "we very soon took three prizes [captured ships] and carried them up to Port-au-Prince," he recalled.[5]

Another privateer captured a ship that carried passengers on their way to England. Louisa Wells was on board, sailing from South Carolina. Her family was loyal to the British king, and she was trying to escape from the bitter conditions she had experienced as a Tory. As she recalled the ship's capture:

> a Gun was fired to bring to, it flashed, a second was fired, and the ball went through our rigging. They then hailed us ...

hoisted out a boat, which was well manned to take us, *as a prize. . . .* at that moment a Volley of Musketry was poured on the deck. . . . The shot whistled over the passengers' heads, upon which they came below, not willing to leave this World.[6]

Soon enough the ship was boarded and the cargo bound for Europe became the property of the Patriots. This type of harassment was maddening to the British, even if it proved to be of little significance. Whenever they could, the British navy took the privateers out of action and imprisoned the crews.

TAKEN PRISONER

Fifteen-year-old James Forten was aboard a privateer, the *Royal Louis,* when it was captured by the British. James, who was born free, was one of twenty blacks in the privateer's crew of two hundred who became prisoners of war. His fate seemed certain: the British usually sent captured black Patriots to the West Indies, where they were sold into slavery.

"But his destiny, by a kind Providence, was otherwise," a tribute to him noted many years later. On board the British ship was the captain's teenage son, who admired James's special skills in the game of marbles, which the two often played. They became friends, and the captain's son persuaded his father to take James to England to be educated and live a life of wealth. James, however, adamantly refused the offer, saying, "I am here a prisoner for the liberties of my country: *I never, NEVER shall prove a traitor to her interests!*"[7]

James Forten eventually was sent to a notorious hulk of a ship known as the *Jersey,* moored off New York. This converted vessel was the worst of several rotting ships that the British used as floating prisons. They were filthy, airless chambers of horror, with no sanitary facilities and crammed with sickly men, many suffering from smallpox. Hundreds of Patriots died on these ships, although James and many others survived to tell their tales.

Thomas Dring, who had shipped out on a privateer, was captured and imprisoned on the *Jersey* late in the Revolution. He wrote of the "unspeakable sufferings" of American prisoners: "emaciated beings . . . their garments hanging in tatters around their meager limbs, and the hue of death upon their careworn faces." Some who were forced into the lower dungeon of the ship "were covered with dirt and filth; their long hair and beards matted and foul." Dring was released during a prisoner exchange between the Americans and British, a moment that he described as "the happiest of my life. . . . I could not refrain from bursting into tears of joy."[8]

BACK ON THE LAND

Back on land, the war in the South during the 1780s was approaching a fateful turn. Washington contemplated how the French navy could be used to help deliver supplies to his troops, which were on the verge of giving up the fight. Meantime, the British commander Charles Cornwallis directed Colonel Banastre Tarleton to attack the American troops at The Cowpens in South Carolina.

As Tarleton advanced, he saw the American force under the command of Brigadier General Daniel Morgan in a defensive line at the edge of the woods. Tarleton approached in a classic bayonet attack—that is, ready to thrust at the defensive line of Rebel soldiers. The British officer did not realize that Morgan had arranged his troops in a new pattern. Morgan placed the inexperienced fighters in a front line and kept the adept Virginia militia in a line slightly behind and hidden in the trees.

When the British attacked, the raw recruits broke and

ran, which Tarleton expected. But once the redcoats had passed the first line of defense, the sharpshooting Virginians fired two deadly volleys at the advancing troops.

At the same time, a cavalry force under the command of Colonel William Washington (a relative of General Washington) came roaring out from behind the Virginians to engage the redcoats in the rear. The frontline Patriot recruits who had retreated turned and came in from another direction. The British were surrounded, and the battle was fought in close quarters. At one point, Colonel Washington was nearly cut down by a redcoat's sword, but a small black boy (his name is unknown), who might have been a bugler or waiter, rode up on horseback and shot the redcoat with a pistol, saving Washington's life.

On January 17, 1781, General Daniel Morgan's sharpshooting riflemen cut down many of the redcoats pursuing them at the Battle of Cowpens.

John Shaw, by then a seasoned veteran of the British army, was part of that battle also. He explained other grim details of the clash:

> The ground was instantly covered with the bodies of the killed and wounded, and a total rout ensued. Not less than 400 of the British infantry were either killed, wounded or taken prisoners.
>
> In this engagement colonel Washington, who commanded a small detachment of American cavalry, had an opportunity of displaying his personal valour in a combat with colonel Tarleton, in which he cut off two of Tarleton's fingers & would have cut off his head, had it not been for his stock-buckle, which deadened the force of the stroke, and saved the life of the British officer.[9]

The British commander Cornwallis was deeply distressed at the loss of life. John Shaw recollected, "I myself was an eyewitness when at that first interview between him and Tarleton, the account of the disaster brought tears from Cornwallis's eyes."[10]

THE BEGINNING OF THE END

The British set up winter camps that year with very few supplies and questioned what they would do come spring. Back in England, the island nation was becoming more and more isolated. The British had no allies and they found themselves in a state of war with America, France, Spain, and Holland. Even their powerful navy was hard-pressed to maintain an advantage in so many theaters of conflict.

Spring brought a few victories to the British in skirmishes around South Carolina, but the toll on men and equipment continued to rise, and Cornwallis could not capture

Greene and the southern troops he commanded. The British commander in chief eventually took his army to the coast and then north to Virginia, giving up on all the areas he had once controlled in the Carolinas. He planned to take Yorktown, Virginia, in the beginning of a new offensive. But by this time, the French navy was at full strength and it was headed for Chesapeake Bay.

Washington had planned to attack New York but changed the direction of his campaign once he learned that Cornwallis's army was taking up a position on the peninsula at Yorktown. He persuaded the French navy to drive the British ships out of the Chesapeake, so that the British troops would have no means of escape. Then Washington rushed his army and some French forces overland to set up a siege of the surrounded redcoats.

A DECISIVE BATTLE

The siege began on September 6, 1781, and Joseph Martin was there. He helped dig trenches to protect the soldiers from stray balls and bullets of the British forces, and he also helped destroy two small British forts. With pickaxes and shovels in hand, Joseph and a crew broke through the fort walls. The French and American troops, with guns blazing, crashed inside, the British retreating before them.

Many were killed or wounded on both sides. But the destruction of the forts, the siege of thirteen days, and the blockade of the sea by the French fleet led to Cornwallis's inevitable decision to surrender. Lemuel Cook, who had enlisted in the Rebel forces when he was sixteen and had been in many skirmishes, was part of Washington's army that day—October 19, 1781. He recalled, "Washington ordered that there should be no laughing at the British; said it was bad enough to have to surrender without being insulted."[11]

*General Washington inspecting the French
batteries during the siege of Yorktown*

The insult was there nonetheless. With the defeat of Cornwallis's army, the fighting throughout the colonies was almost over. There were some skirmishes, and the British navy defeated the French navy in a decisive battle in the Caribbean Islands, but the British will was broken. A new government came to power in London, and negotiations were started to end all English rule in the United States of America. On September 3, 1783, a treaty was finally signed between England and its former enemies, the United States, France, and Spain. Part of that treaty provided for U.S. independence from Great Britain.

On that happy day "when peace was declared," recalled Patriot fighter Sam Downing, "we burnt thirteen candles in every hut, one for each State."[12]

Source Notes

One

1. Quoted in Leslie H. Fishel, Jr., and Benjamin Quarles, *The Negro American: A Documentary History* (Glenview, Ill.: Scott, Foresman and Company, 1967), 46.

2. Joseph Plumb Martin, *Private Yankee Doodle: Being a Narrative of Some of the Adventures, Dangers and Sufferings of a Revolutionary Soldier*, ed. George F. Scheer (Boston: Little, Brown and Company, 1962), 16.

3. Ibid., 17.

4. Ibid., xii.

5. Quoted in Fishel and Quarles, *Negro American*, 49.

Two

1. Lydia Minturn Post, *Personal Recollections of the American Revolution: A Private Journal*, ed. Sidney Barclay (Port Washington, N.Y.: Kennikat Press, 1970), 21.

2. Elizabeth Lichtenstein Johnston, *Recollections of a Georgia Loyalist*, ed. Arthur Wentworth Eaton (New York: M. F. Mansfield and Co., 1901), 44.

3. Quoted in Eric F. Goldman, "Firebrands of the Revolution," *National Geographic*, July 1974, 18.

4. Quoted in Beverly J. Armento et. al., *A More Perfect Union* (Boston: Houghton Mifflin, 1991), 664–665.

5. Jeremiah Greenman, *Diary of a Common Soldier in the American Revolution, 1775–1783*, eds. Robert C. Bray and Paul E. Bushnell (DeKalb, Ill.: Northern Illinois University Press, 1978), 266.

6. Quoted in Francis G. Walett, *Patriots, Loyalists and Printers* (Worcester, Mass.: American Antiquarian Society, 1976), 88.

Three

1. John Greenwood, *A Young Patriot in the American Revolution* (Tyrone, Pa.: Westvaco, 1981), 59–60.

2. Quoted in Richard Wheeler, *Voices of 1776* (New York: Thomas Y. Crowell, 1972), 72.

3. Ibid.

4. Benjamin Tallmadge, *Memoir of Colonel Benjamin Tallmadge* (New York: Arno Press, 1968), 9–10.

5. Enoch Anderson, *Personal Recollections of Captain Enoch Anderson* (New York: Arno Press, 1971), 21–22.

6. Tallmadge, *Memoir*, 11–13.

7. Post, *Personal Recollections*, 17–18.

8. Anderson, *Personal Recollections*, 28.

9. Quoted in Henry Steele Commager and Richard B. Morris, eds., *The Spirit of 'Seventy-Six* (New York: Bonanza Books, 1983), 507.

10. Greenwood, *Young Patriot*, 82–84.

11. Quoted in Commager and Morris, *Spirit of 'Seventy-Six*, 519–520.

12. Ibid., 520.

13. Greenman, *Diary*, 73.

14. Ebenezer Fletcher, *The Narrative of Ebenezer Fletcher, A Soldier of the Revolution, Written by Himself* (1827; reprint, 4th ed., Freeport, N.Y.: Books for Libraries, 1970), 12–15.

Four

1. John Robert Shaw, *A Narrative of the Life and Travels of John Robert Shaw, The Well-Digger, Now Resident in Lexington, Kentucky* (Lexington, Ky.: Daniel Bradford, 1807), 22.

2. Ibid., 25.

3. Bruce E. Burgoyne, ed. and trans., *Diaries of a Hessian Chaplain and the Chaplain's Assistant* (Pennsauken, N.J.: Johannes Schwalm Historical Association, 1990), 23.

4. Ibid., 25.

5. Ray W. Pettengill, trans., *Letters From America 1776–1779 Being Letters of Brunswick, Hessian, and Waldeck Officers With the British Armies During the Revolution* (Port Washington, N.Y.: Kennikat Press, 1924), 97.

6. Marvin L. Brown, Jr., trans., *Baroness von Riedesel and the American Revolution: Journal and Correspondence of a Tour of Duty 1776–1783* (Chapel Hill, N.C.: University of North Carolina Press, 1965), 55. Also quoted in Wheeler, *Voices of 1776*, 243.

7. Shaw, *Life and Travels*, 60–62.

8. Ibid., 62.

9. Ibid., 63.

Five

1. Post, *Personal Recollections*, 26.

2. Sarah Wister, *The Journal and Occasional Writings of Sarah Wister*, ed. Kathryn Zabelle Derounian (Cranbury, N.J.: Associated University Press, 1987), 44.

3. Margaret Morris, *Private Journal* (1836; microfiche, typed copy of original, Washington, D.C.: Library of Congress).

4. Johnston, *Recollections*, 46–47.

5. Grace Growden Galloway, *Diary of Grace Growden Galloway* (New York: Arno Press, 1971), 52.

6. Post, *Personal Recollections*, 29–30.

7. Ibid., 31.

8. Ibid., 32.

Six

1. Quoted in Commager and Morris, *Spirit of 'Seventy-Six*, 1152.

2. "Oliver De Lancey's Journal of the Pennsylvania Mutiny," appendix to *Mutiny in January* by Carl Van Doren (New York: Viking Press, 1943), 248.

3. Elias Brewster Hillard, *The Last Men of the Revolution,* ed. Wendell D. Garrett (1864; reprint, Barre, Mass.: Barre Publishers, 1968), 63.

4. Greenwood, *Young Patriot,* 115.

5. Ibid., 116.

6. Louisa Susannah Wells, *The Journal of a Voyage From Charlestown to London Undertaken During the American Revolution by a Daughter of an Eminent American Loyalist in the Year 1778 and Written From Memory Only in 1779* (1906; reprint, New York: New York Times and Arno Press, 1968), 6–7.

7. Robert Purvis, "James Forten (a eulogy on his life and character, delivered at Bethel Church, Philadelphia, March 30, 1842)," abridged and reprinted in *The Colored Patriots of the American Revolution,* ed. William C. Nell (New York: Arno Press and New York Times, 1968), 168.

8. Thomas Dring, *Recollections of the "Jersey" Prison Ship,* in *America Rebels: Narratives of the Patriots,* ed. Richard M. Dorson (New York: Pantheon, 1953), 74, 88.

9. Shaw, *Life and Travels,* 55.

10. Ibid.

11. Hillard, *Last Men,* 63.

12. Ibid., 37.

Further Reading

American Heritage Illustrated History of the United States, Vol. 3: The Revolution. Westbury, N.Y.: Choice Pub NY, 1988. Reprint 1963 edition.

Bliven, Bruce, Jr. *American Revolution.* New York: Random House, 1963.

Carter, Alden R. *The American Revolution: War for Independence.* New York: Franklin Watts, 1993.

Davis, Burke. *Black Heroes of the American Revolution.* San Diego: Harcourt Brace, 1992.

De Pauw, Linda G. *Founding Mothers: Women of America in the Revolutionary Era.* Boston: Houghton Mifflin, 1975.

Dudley, William, ed. *The American Revolution: Opposing Viewpoints.* San Diego: Greenhaven, 1992.

Hughes, Libby. *Valley Forge.* New York: Dillon Press, 1993.

Kent, Deborah. *The American Revolution: Give Me Liberty, or Give Me Death!* Hillside, N.J.: Enslow, 1994.

Marrin, Albert. *The War for Independence: The Story of the American Revolution.* New York: Atheneum, 1988.

McPhillips, Martin. *The Battle of Trenton.* Morristown, N.J.: Silver Burdett, 1984.

Meltzer, Milton. *The American Revolutionaries: A History in Their Own Words.* New York: HarperCollins, 1987.

———. *The American Revolutionaries: A History in Their Own Words, 1750–1800.* New York: HarperCollins, 1993.

Merrill, Arthur A. *Battle of White Plains.* Haverford, Pa.: Analysis, 1976.

Minks, Louise, and Benton Minks. *The Revolutionary War.* New York: Facts on File, 1992.

Morris, Richard B. *The American Revolution.* Minneapolis: Lerner, 1985. Revised edition.

Nordstrom, Judy. *Concord and Lexington.* New York: Dillon, 1993.

Olesky, Walter. *Boston Tea Party.* New York: Franklin Watts, 1993.

Smith, Carter, ed. *The Revolutionary War: A Sourcebook on Colonial America.* Brookfield, Conn.: Millbrook Press, 1991.

Stewart, Gail. *The Revolutionary War.* San Diego: Lucent, 1991.

Zall, P. M. , ed. *Becoming American: Young People in the American Revolution.* Hamden, Conn.: Linnet, 1993.

Index

Adams, Samuel, 17–18
Arnold, Benedict, 24
Attucks, Crispus, 7

Bennington, Battle of, 35
blacks
    enlistment of, 13–14
    as prisoners of war, 51
Boston, 8, 10, 13, 22–23, 24, 29,
    50
Boston Massacre, 7, 17
Brandywine, Battle of, 35
Breed's Hill, Battle of, 13
Britain, 9, 15, 44, 49, 56
British, 9, 13, 17, 23, 32
    conflicts with other nations, 54
    end of rule over colonies, 56
    and enlisting blacks, 13–14
    forces, 13, 22, 25, 26, 31, 35,
        37, 41, 46, 51, 54, 56. *See*
      also redcoats
    and Indians, 40
    Royal Army, 32, 33
    rule, 9, 15, 18, 19
British East India Company, 8
Bunker Hill, Battle of, 13, 22–23
Burgoyne, "Gentleman
    Johnny," 34–36

Canada, 16, 23, 25, 30, 43
Caribbean Islands, Battle of, 56

Charleston, Battle of, 38
Chesapeake Bay, Battle of, 55
Clark, George Rogers, 40
Common Sense, 18
Concord, Battle of, 11, 13, 22
Continental Congresses, 10, 12,
    13, 23, 49
Continental forces, 13, 23, 25,
    30–31, 34, 38, 45, 48, 50, 52
Cornwallis, Charles, 52, 54
Cowpens, Battle of, 52–53

Declaration of Independence,
    14, 15, 20
Delaware River, 27
diseases plaguing troops, 35, 30,
    37, 52

Fort Ticonderoga, 31, 35
Fort Ticonderoga, Battle of, 35
French
    as ally of Patriots, 36–38, 40
    forces, 49, 52, 55, 56
friction within families, 15–16

Gates, Horatio, 35

Hale, Nathan, 31
Henry, Patrick, 17, 18
Hessian soldiers, 27, 29, 33,
    41

independence treaty signed, 56
Indians, 23, 34, 40

Jersey, the, 51, 52

King George III, 10

Lexington, Battle of, 11, 13, 22
Long Island, 46
Long Island, Battle of, 25–26
Loyalists. *See* Tories

Morristown, 30, 34, 48

New England, 7, 25, 34, 40
New Jersey, 25–27, 30
New York, 25, 31, 33–35, 50, 51, 55
Northwest Territory, 40

Quebec, Battle of, 23–24

Paine, Thomas, 17–19
Patriots, 8, 18, 21, 43–44, 51. *See also* Continental forces
   enlistment of militia, 11–12
   militia, 10, 12, 13, 18, 22, 48, 52
   minutemen, 10–11
Princeton, Battle of, 30
privateers, 49–51

Quebec, 23, 24

reasons for war, 7–11
   Boston Massacre, 7, 17
   Boston Tea party, 8, 18

British cutting off supplies, 20
   closing of Boston Harbor, 8
   unfair taxing of colonists, 7–8, 18
Rebels. *See* Patriots
redcoats, 21, 27, 33, 38–40, 53, 55
   enlistment of, 32–33
Revere, Paul, 10

Saratoga, Battle of, 35, 36
Shaw, John, 32, 38, 39, 54
Sons of Liberty, 17

Tories, 16, 23, 34, 38, 40, 43, 44, 50
Trenton, Battle of, 27–29

Valley Forge, 37, 48

Washington, George, 13, 22, 23, 25–27, 29, 30, 37, 48, 49, 52–55
Washington, William, 53
Wheatley, Phillis, 19
women
   at home, 38–39, 40, 44–46
   traveling with army, 23–24, 35–36
Woodhull, General Nathaniel, 46–47

"Yankee Doodle," 22
Yorktown, Battle of, 55